MAKING AND SELLING SUBSCRIPTION BOXES FROM SCRATCH

The Subscription Box Playbook: Strategies For Creating, Marketing, And Scaling Your Business

SYBIL WHITNEY

Copyright © SYBIL WHITNEY 2024

All rights reserved. No part of this publication may be reproduced, distributed, or transmitted in any form or by any means, including photocopying, recording, or other electronic or mechanical methods, without the prior written permission of the author, except in the case of brief quotations embodied in critical reviews and certain other noncommercial uses permitted by copyright law.

Disclaimer:

The information provided in this book, is intended for general informational purposes only and should not be considered as professional advice.

The author has made every effort to ensure the accuracy of the information presented. However, readers are advised to consult with a qualified healthcare professional before attempting any herbal remedies or making significant changes to their wellness routine. Individual health conditions vary, and what may be suitable for one person may not be appropriate for another.

It is important to note that the author is not in any endorsement deal, partnership, or affiliation with any organization, brand, or company mentioned in this book. Any references to specific products or services are based on the author's personal experience or general knowledge and do not imply an endorsement or promotion of those products or services.

Contents

CHAPTER ONE 11
A SUBSCRIPTION BOX: WHAT IS IT? 11
Subscription Box Types 11
The Advantages Of Launching A Subscription Box Company 13

CHAPTER TWO 17
IDENTIFYING YOUR NICHE 17
Finding Your Area Of Interest And Proficiency 17
Finding The Target Audience Through Market Research 18
Assessing The Competition And Identifying Market Gaps 19

CHAPTER THREE 21
ORGANIZING YOUR BOX 21
Choosing Your Subscription Box's Theme 21
Selecting Items That Suit Your Specialization 22
Developing A Pricing Strategy And Budget 24

CHAPTER FOUR 27
PURCHASING GOODS 27
Locating Vendors And Suppliers 27

    Getting Discounts And Deals Negotiated 28

    Taking Care Of Product Consistency And Quality 29

CHAPTER FIVE 31

    CREATING YOUR BOX 31

        Making Visually Appealing Packaging 31

        Personalizing Box Inserts And Adding Logos 32

        Shipping And Handling Packaging Considerations 33

CHAPTER SIX 35

    CREATING YOUR WEBSITE 35

        Selecting A Platform For Your Online Business 35

        Creating A Website That Is Easy To Use 36

        Configuring Security And Payment Gateways 38

CHAPTER SEVEN 41

    OVERSIGHT OF SUBSCRIPTION 41

        Configuring A System For Subscription Management 41

        Responding To Consumer Questions And Suggestions 43

        Controlling Stock And Delivery Procedures 45

CHAPTER EIGHT 49

GROWING YOUR ENTERTAINMENT 49

   Data And Metric Analysis for Growth 49

   Adding New Box Variations Or Increasing Product Offerings 51

   Expanding Activities Without Compromising Quality Or Customer Contentment 53

CHAPTER NINE 57

   FAQS AND REGULAR QUESTIONS 57

   What Should I Do About Shipment Problems? 57

   What Happens If Subscribers Wish To Stop? 59

   How Should Refunds And Returns Be Handled? .. 60

   How Can I Successfully Manage My Inventory? .. 64

CONCERNING THIS BOOK

When starting a subscription box business, prospective entrepreneurs might use the book "Guide to Making and Selling Subscription Boxes From Scratch" as an invaluable guide.

It is critical to comprehend the fundamentals of subscription boxes, which is why this article painstakingly explains what they are, the variety of kinds they cover, and the numerous advantages they provide to startups. The book starts with the fundamental step of identifying your specialty.

To carve out a distinctive niche in the market, it argues for a methodical approach, advising entrepreneurs to identify their passion and competence, undertake in-depth market research, and detect their target audience.

A crucial part of the process is Planning Your Box, which explains the nuances of choosing a theme that aligns with your brand's values, carefully choosing products that are specific to your market, and creating a budget and price plan that will support long-term growth.

Product sourcing is an art, and this guide provides priceless advice on locating trustworthy suppliers, negotiating contracts skillfully, and guaranteeing consistent product quality—a vital component of client happiness.

Designing Your Box is a book that helps entrepreneurs create visually appealing packaging, customize inserts for brand reinforcement, and handle packaging considerations for easy shipping and handling. It's where style and practicality come together.

Creating a strong online presence is essential, and the chapter on creating a website is a gold mine of information that covers everything from choosing an e-commerce platform to strengthening it with strong security features and a user-friendly design.

Any company's attempt needs marketing and promotion, and this guide covers every aspect of efficient marketing methods, from creating a thorough plan to using influencer relationships and social media to draw in and keep subscribers.

Handling client inquiries and feedback, setting up subscription management systems, and expertly coordinating inventory and delivery procedures are just a few of the ways this book makes managing subscriptions a logistical ballet easier.

The ultimate goal is to scale your business, and this guide gives business owners the skills they need to do so while maintaining uncompromising quality and customer happiness.

It covers data analysis, product offers expansion and operational scaling. A compass for navigating the many obstacles that come with operating a subscription box business, such as managing inventory and shipping concerns, is provided by FAQs and Common Concerns.

Essentially, the book acts as a thorough road map, enabling business owners to start their subscription box journey with conviction, clarity, and confidence.

CHAPTER ONE

A SUBSCRIPTION BOX: WHAT IS IT?

A subscription box is a carefully selected assortment of goods that consumers pay a certain amount to receive regularly, usually once a month.

These boxes, which are centered around a particular theme or hobby, might include anything from books and fitness equipment to snacks and cosmetics.

Subscription boxes are popular because they provide customers with a sense of surprise and convenience. Without having to deal with the inconvenience of shopping around, they give people the chance to find new products that are catered to their interests.

Subscription Box Types

There are many different kinds of subscription boxes available to suit a wide range of interests and tastes. Typical varieties include some of the following:

Beauty & skincare boxes: These boxes typically include skincare items, makeup, and beauty equipment that are carefully chosen to fit a variety of skin types and preferences. Samples or full-sized products may be given to customers to test out.

Food & Snack Boxes: Meal kits, gourmet snacks, and artisanal delicacies are delivered to subscribers' doorsteps in food subscription boxes.

These kits can accommodate certain dietary needs, such as gluten-free, vegan, or keto.

Book Subscription Boxes: Readers can sign up to receive a box of carefully chosen books based on their reading tastes. These crates might also contain books-related accessories and goods.

Fitness and Wellness Boxes: To help subscribers reach their fitness and wellness objectives, these boxes include products for self-care, healthy foods, vitamins, and training equipment.

Pet subscription boxes: Monthly boxes filled with toys, snacks, and grooming supplies allow pet owners to spoil their four-legged companions.

Depending on the size and tastes of the pet, these boxes are frequently altered.

Subscription boxes for a "lifestyle": These boxes include a variety of goods from home décor, fashion accessories, electronics, and stationery. They serve people looking for a well-chosen assortment of fashionable or unusual goods.

The Advantages Of Launching A Subscription Box Company

For entrepreneurs, launching a subscription box business can have a lot of advantages:

recurrent Revenue: Since subscribers sign up for monthly or yearly subscriptions, subscription models offer a steady and recurrent stream of income. Over time, the stability and expansion of the company may be aided by this consistent source of revenue.

Customer Loyalty: Subscription box companies can cultivate enduring relationships with their members by providing curated boxes that are customized to each subscriber's tastes.

Customers are more inclined to stick with the items and renew their subscriptions if they feel that they are getting value out of them and like the element of surprise.

Minimal Overhead: Since subscription box companies don't need physical storefronts or significant stocks, their overhead expenses are frequently lower than those of typical retail establishments.

This can make starting their own subscription box business with little initial capital easier for would-be business owners.

Market Differentiation: Subscription boxes allow companies to establish a specialized market inside particular sectors or hobbies. Subscriber box companies can stand out from rivals and draw in a devoted clientele by catering to specialized markets and providing distinctive, hand-picked experiences.

Data-driven Insights: Companies that provide subscription boxes have access to useful information on the tastes, spending patterns, and feedback of their clients.

Businesses can choose wisely when it comes to future enhancements to the subscriber experience, marketing tactics, and product selection by evaluating this data.

Aspiring business owners wishing to get into this booming industry must grasp the idea behind subscription boxes, investigate the different kinds that are out there, and appreciate the advantages of launching a subscription box company.

Subscription box companies can prosper and expand in the current competitive market by capitalizing on consumers' needs for convenience, exploration, and customization.

CHAPTER TWO

IDENTIFYING YOUR NICHE

Finding Your Area Of Interest And Proficiency

It's important to start with what you know and love while exploring the world of subscription box services. Think about your interests, pastimes, and areas of expertise for a while. What excites you? What could you converse endlessly about? You're setting the stage for a subscription box that appeals to both you and potential customers by identifying these core interests.

Think about your special abilities and expertise. Do you have a passion for skincare? A fitness expert? A voracious reader? Any of these passions, and more, might be the focus of your subscription box. Your enthusiasm will propel your company along, igniting your inventiveness and commitment as you curate boxes that thrill your subscribers every month.

Finding The Target Audience Through Market Research

After determining your area of skill and enthusiasm, it's necessary to thoroughly research your target market. Who are the individuals with similar interests to yours? Which demographics are they in? Where do they congregate both in person and online? By getting to know your target market, you can customize your subscription box to suit their requirements and tastes.

Use internet resources and tools to compile information on customer trends and behavior in your industry. Online polls, industry forums, and social media sites can all offer insightful information about the features that prospective subscribers to your box service are searching for. To optimize appeal and improve your products, pay attention to their preferences and feedback.

Assessing The Competition And Identifying Market Gaps

Regardless of how specialized your interests are, there is probably already some competition in the market for subscription boxes.

However, don't let it stop you. Rather, take advantage of the chance to assess what's already available and pinpoint any holes that your distinctive solution may close.

Look closely at who your rivals are. What do they excel at doing? In what areas are they lacking? Are there any underutilized market niches that you might pursue?

You may position your subscription box service to stand out and draw in new customers by evaluating the advantages and disadvantages of the current market players.

Seek out chances to be creative and set your subscription box apart from the competitors. Discovering your market niche will put you on the road to success, whether it's through distinctive product offerings, individualized customization choices, or first-rate customer service.

CHAPTER THREE

ORGANIZING YOUR BOX

Choosing Your Subscription Box's Theme

The success of your subscription box depends on the theme you choose. Your topic should appeal to and represent the interests and preferences of your target audience.

Investigate current trends in your industry to find any openings or gaps that you may take advantage of. Think about topics that are particular enough to set your box apart from competitors, but also broad enough to appeal to a large audience.

During this phase, brainstorming sessions can be quite beneficial. Get your group together or ask friends and coworkers for suggestions and ideas. Consider what makes your subscription box special and what special benefits you can provide to subscribers. Take into account elements that can inspire themed boxes and keep your offers current and relevant, such as seasonality, holidays, or special events.

After you've selected a few, test them out with a focus group or survey to see what people are interested in and get feedback.

Seek themes that elicit a sense of enthusiasm and excitement in your intended audience. Keep in mind that choosing a theme will determine how your subscription box experience is overall, so pick carefully.

Selecting Items That Suit Your Specialization

Making the correct product choices for your subscription box is crucial to satisfying your clients and winning them over as repeat customers. Determine your niche and the unique requirements and preferences of your target market before anything else. When choosing products, keep things like age, gender, interests, and lifestyle in mind.

Look into possible merchants and providers to locate premium goods that fit your concept and satisfy your clients. Seek out distinctive and cutting-edge products that provide subscribers with value and utility.

To add a personal touch and help your neighborhood, think about collaborating with nearby small businesses or craftsmen.

When selecting products for your subscription box, variety is essential. Provide a variety of regular products, exclusives, and limited edition items to keep subscribers interested and anticipating each delivery.

To improve the whole unboxing experience and evoke a sense of excitement and anticipation, pay attention to the presentation and packaging of the products.

Developing A Pricing Strategy And Budget

A well-defined budget and pricing strategy are important for guaranteeing the financial sustainability of your subscription box enterprise. First, figure out how much it will cost you to buy the goods, package it, ship it, and advertise it. When estimating your monthly or quarterly budget, take into account both fixed and variable costs.

Determine your price plan based on market research, competitor analysis, and client feedback once you have a firm grasp of your costs. When determining your prices, take into account elements including pricing tiers, perceived value, and subscriber retention. Be open and honest about your pricing, and make sure prospective customers understand the advantages and worth of your subscription package.

Try out various price structures, like tiers or discounts for extended memberships, to determine the best ratio between cost and return on investment. Keep a careful eye on your pricing plan and be ready to make any necessary adjustments in response to client feedback and market conditions.

Recall that the objective is to present a strong value proposition that persuades clients to sign up and continue their subscriptions over time.

CHAPTER FOUR

PURCHASING GOODS

Locating Vendors And Suppliers

Choosing the appropriate vendors and suppliers is essential to the success of your subscription box company. To begin, do extensive web research using resources such as Alibaba, ThomasNet, or Google. Find vendors who sell the goods you wish to put in your boxes.

Contact the suppliers on your list to find out more about their offerings, costs, and minimum order quantities (MOQs). Never be afraid to request samples to evaluate the products' quality directly.

Moreover, networking can be a useful resource for locating suppliers. Join online forums or groups that are relevant to your niche, go to trade exhibits, and attend industry events. Other business owners are frequently happy to recommend their reliable providers.

Getting Discounts And Deals Negotiated

You may minimize money and boost your profit margins by negotiating discounts and deals with suppliers. Establish positive working relationships with your vendors first.

Demonstrate to them your commitment to a long-term collaboration and your seriousness about conducting business with them.

Be ready to use variables like exclusivity agreements, payment terms, or volume discounts as leverage during negotiations. Draw attention to the possibility of recurring business and stress the importance of a win-win collaboration.

If the terms are not acceptable, don't be scared to leave. There are many different vendors available, and occasionally deciding to move on can result in better offers.

Taking Care Of Product Consistency And Quality

Retaining customers and establishing a solid brand reputation depends on maintaining product quality and consistency. Make sure the products from vendors fulfill your requirements by carefully vetting them before concluding agreements.

Ask for product samples, then give them a thorough testing run to make sure they live up to your standards. This includes evaluating elements including general presentation, packaging, and durability.

After choosing your suppliers, set up precise procedures for quality control. This can entail routinely going through incoming inventory to look for flaws or irregularities.

Make sure your vendors understand your expectations, and when problems do occur, work together to find solutions.

To make sure your consumers are satisfied with the products in your subscription boxes, ask them for feedback regularly. Proceed with future product and sourcing decisions with this feedback in hand.

CHAPTER FIVE

CREATING YOUR BOX

Making Visually Appealing Packaging

The packaging of subscription boxes makes a first impression. It's what entices subscribers and gives them a sense of anticipation for their monthly bundle. For this reason, designing visually appealing packaging is essential to the success of your subscription box company.

Start by thinking about your subscription box's theme and target market. Your packaging should convey your subscribers' interests and sense of style. To stand out from the crowd and attract attention, use vivid colors, strong visuals, and original designs. Consider how you may strengthen your brand identification by incorporating your business's messaging and emblem into the packaging.

It is imperative to take into account the functional aspects of your packaging alongside its visual appeal. Make sure it's easy for subscribers to open and sturdy enough to safeguard the contents throughout shipping. To attract customers who care about the environment and lessen your carbon footprint, think about utilizing eco-friendly materials.

Personalizing Box Inserts And Adding Logos

Another way to improve the subscriber experience and bolster your brand is to personalize box inserts. To make subscribers feel valued and special, think about including personalized comments or remarks. Additionally, you can include branded postcards, stickers, or other promotional products that fit nicely with the subscription box's theme.

Consider how your box inserts will enhance the whole unboxing experience when you create them. For instance, you may provide special discounts or promotions for further purchases, or you may give advice or instructions on how to use the things inside the box. Creating a fun and unique experience that entices users to return month after month is the aim.

Shipping And Handling Packaging Considerations

It is crucial to think about how your box will fare in shipment and handling while constructing it. Select robust materials like padded envelopes or corrugated cardboard that can endure the demands of shipping. To stop damage and leaks, reinforce edges and seams.

You'll need to think about the practicalities of shipping in addition to safeguarding the contents of your box. To minimize shipping expenses, make sure your packaging is both lightweight and robust enough to safeguard delicate objects.

To expedite shipment and cut down on packaging waste, think about implementing uniform packaging sizes.

Labeling and branding are important considerations. Ensure that your firm name, logo, and return address are prominently displayed on the labels of your boxes. To guarantee that your packages are handled carefully while in transit, think about attaching fragile stickers or handling instructions. You can guarantee the safe and elegant delivery of your subscription boxes by taking these packing tips into account.

CHAPTER SIX

CREATING YOUR WEBSITE

Selecting A Platform For Your Online Business

It's critical to choose the appropriate platform for your subscription box business. There are numerous choices, each with advantages and disadvantages of its own. Take into account elements like cost, scalability, customization possibilities, simplicity of use, and tool integration.

Well-known e-commerce platforms with features designed specifically for subscription-based enterprises include Shopify, WooCommerce, and BigCommerce. For example, Shopify is a well-liked option for business owners due to its user-friendly interface, numerous app connections, and customizable themes. Conversely, WooCommerce is an open-source WordPress plugin that provides scalability and flexibility to companies of all kinds. BigCommerce distinguishes itself with its sophisticated marketing tools and integrated subscription features.

Examine each platform in light of your financial situation and unique demands. To improve customer experience and streamline operations, look for capabilities like marketing automation, inventory tracking, and subscription management.

Creating A Website That Is Easy To Use

Since your website serves as the public face of your subscription box company, user experience design is crucial.

Establish a layout that accurately represents your business identity and is clear and eye-catching. To highlight your items and subscription plans, use eye-catching photos and interesting text.

Make sure that the calls to action on your website are obvious and point them in the direction of subscription alternatives and product specifics.

Make good use of search options and user-friendly menus to assist people in finding what they're looking for quickly.

Make your website mobile-friendly to attract visitors who prefer to browse and shop on tablets and smartphones.

Your website will appear and work flawlessly on all screen sizes thanks to responsive design, which also improves user experience and increases conversions.

To answer frequently asked questions and give visitors the knowledge they need to make educated purchases, think about introducing tools like live chat assistance or FAQ sections.

Configuring Security And Payment Gateways

It is crucial to secure online transactions if you want to gain your consumers' confidence and reputation. Select trustworthy payment gateways that accept a range of payment options and provide strong security measures.

You may safely take credit card payments with platforms like Shopify and WooCommerce that link with top payment processors like PayPal, Stripe, and Square. Sensitive consumer data is encrypted by these gateways to prevent fraud and illegal access.

Use SSL encryption in addition to safe payment channels to protect data traveling between your website and the browsers of your clients.

By establishing a secure connection, SSL certificates guarantee the privacy and protection of critical data, including credit card numbers, from online dangers.

Update the security software and protocols on your website regularly to reduce risks and stay ahead of potential vulnerabilities.

To protect the financial information of your clients and your company, keep an eye out for unusual activity in transactions and put fraud protection procedures in place. By placing a high priority on security, you may develop a loyal customer base by establishing your subscription box brand's credibility.

CHAPTER SEVEN

OVERSIGHT OF SUBSCRIPTION

Configuring A System For Subscription Management

To effectively manage customer subscriptions and handle the influx of orders, a subscription management system must be set up. To streamline processes, choosing the appropriate software or platform is one of the essential elements in this process. There are numerous platforms for managing subscriptions that offer diverse features and functionality. It's crucial to select one that fits the objectives and demands of your company.

Configuring a platform by your subscription model comes next after selecting one. This includes establishing pricing structures, billing cycles, and subscription plans. Payment gateway integration is also required to enable smooth transactions and set up automatic recurring payments.

Moreover, a good user experience depends on having a customer site where users can update payment details, manage their accounts, and change their subscription preferences. While giving consumers more control over their subscriptions, this self-service option can lighten your workload.

Another crucial component of running a subscription-based business is routinely tracking and evaluating subscription metrics. Monitoring important performance metrics like subscriber growth, customer lifetime value, and churn rate can provide important information about the state of your company and point up areas for development.

To guarantee seamless operations and client satisfaction, establishing a strong subscription management system requires careful planning, the selection of the appropriate tools, and continual monitoring.

Responding To Consumer Questions And Suggestions

In a subscription-based firm, responding to consumer questions and comments is essential to preserving goodwill and guaranteeing client pleasure. Inquiries should be promptly and politely answered to improve the overall customer experience and foster loyalty.

To accommodate a wide range of consumer preferences, a multi-channel support system must be implemented. This could entail assisting with social media, live chat, phone, or email. Customers' expectations can be managed and annoyance can be decreased by giving clear information on how to contact you for assistance and by establishing reasonable expectations for response times.

To find areas for development and identify pain points, it's imperative to proactively seek feedback from clients in addition to responding to individual requests. Surveys, feedback forms, and even social media polls can be used for this. Examining this input might assist in influencing future service improvements and product offerings by revealing important information about consumer preferences.

Additionally, by putting up a knowledge base or FAQ section on your website, you may enable users to look up answers to frequently asked issues on their own, saving you time and money by allowing staff to focus on more difficult problems.

Finally, providing excellent customer service requires educating customer service agents to respond to queries quickly and sympathetically. By giving support agents with continuous training and tools, we can provide them the information and abilities they need to efficiently handle consumer concerns.

All things considered, companies can promote long-term profitability, enhance customer pleasure, and cultivate great connections by giving priority to consumer questions and feedback.

Controlling Stock And Delivery Procedures

Maintaining appropriate stock levels to meet demand and guaranteeing on-time delivery of subscription boxes depend heavily on inventory management and fulfillment procedures.

Monitoring stock levels, restocking goods as needed, and streamlining storage and warehouse operations are all components of effective inventory management.

By automating reordering procedures, producing reports to evaluate inventory performance, and offering real-time visibility into stock levels, inventory management software can simplify these procedures. This can lessen the chance of lost sales or extra inventory-carrying expenses by preventing stockouts and overstock scenarios.

Furthermore, fulfilling customer expectations for order accuracy and shipment timeliness requires the implementation of effective fulfillment procedures. To reduce mistakes and delays, order picking, packaging, and shipping procedures must be optimized.

By automatically updating stock levels as orders are fulfilled and giving clients real-time tracking information, integrating your inventory management system with your fulfillment procedures helps further optimize operations.

Additionally, maintaining a consistent supply of goods and prompt delivery of subscription boxes requires building connections with dependable suppliers and logistics partners.

Achieving acceptable terms and agreements with suppliers can aid in lowering the risks and expenses related to fulfillment and inventory management.

Optimizing inventory turnover and reducing carrying costs require regular reviews and adjustments of inventory levels based on sales patterns and demand forecasts.

This could entail carrying out recurring audits, examining sales information, modifying lead times, and reordering points as necessary.

For a subscription-based business to run smoothly and provide a satisfying client experience, inventory and fulfillment procedures must be managed effectively. Enterprises may optimize customer happiness, cut expenses, and avoid errors by putting in place effective systems and procedures.

CHAPTER EIGHT

GROWING YOUR ENTERTAINMENT

Data And Metric Analysis for Growth

When your subscription box business takes off, it's critical to look at metrics and data to ensure long-term growth.

Your strategy and decision-making are guided by this analysis, which acts as a compass. Determine the key performance indicators (KPIs) that are pertinent to your company's objectives first. These might include revenue figures, customer feedback scores, acquisition costs, and subscription retention rates.

To efficiently collect and analyze data, make use of analytics solutions like Google Analytics, customer relationship management (CRM) software, or subscription management systems. Monitor consumer behavior, how they interact with your boxes, and how they react to promotional offers. Gaining insight into these analytics will help you spot trends, pinpoint areas that need work, and capitalize on tactics that work.

To remain flexible and sensitive to changes in the market, examine and analyze your data regularly. Keep an eye out for patterns that point to changing consumer preferences or new business prospects. For example, if you observe a surge in interest in a specific product category inside your subscription box, think about modifying your offerings to take advantage of this pattern.

Utilize data to enhance your marketing endeavors as well. Determine which channels work best for bringing in new subscribers, then direct resources in that direction.

You can optimize conversion rates and return on investment by fine-tuning your targeting, marketing, and timing with a data-driven strategy.

Adding New Box Variations Or Increasing Product Offerings

Adding new box types or broadening your product line is a calculated step that will help you expand and meet changing customer demands.

Start by gathering information about the market to find possible areas for expansion. Take into account elements like competition analysis, market demand, and the viability of using your current infrastructure.

Make sure your product line expansions are to the tastes of your target market and your brand identity. Determine whether the new products serve a different market niche from your current offerings or are a complement to them.

If your subscription box is mainly focused on beauty products, for example, you may look into making skincare-specific boxes or seasonal trend-based themed collections.

Strategically roll out new package varieties while considering feedback and client preferences. To increase consumer pleasure and engagement, think about providing limited-edition boxes or personalization possibilities. Work together with suppliers, craftspeople, or influencers to select special goods and experiences that enhance the value of your subscription boxes.

Retain your adaptability and agility when trying out new products. Keep a close eye on client feedback and performance indicators so that you may adjust and improve your product strategy as necessary.

Be willing to change course or stop providing products that don't appeal to your target market or help you achieve your goals.

Expanding Activities Without Compromising Quality Or Customer Contentment

Growing a subscription box business requires scaling processes, but you can't sacrifice quality or client satisfaction in the process. To find opportunities for efficiency improvements and optimization, start by evaluating your present workflows, procedures, and infrastructure.

Invest in automation technologies and scalable tech solutions to eliminate manual labor and streamline operations.

Establish a reliable inventory management system to monitor stock levels, predict demand, and avoid overstocking or stockouts. To increase agility and scalability, use cloud-based software for order fulfillment, shipping, and customer service.

Throughout the scaling process, keep quality control front and center. To guarantee consistency and quality, set strict guidelines and procedures for product sourcing, packaging, and fulfillment. Maintaining quality standards and reducing risks requires routinely auditing your supply chain and vendor relationships.

Put the needs of your customers first while you grow your business. Keep the lines of communication open with subscribers, and take quick action to resolve any problems or concerns that come up.

Give your customers a more individualized experience by adding kind touches like handwritten letters, unexpected presents, or special benefits for loyal members.

Invest in hiring and training staff members who share your brand values and are dedicated to providing outstanding customer service as you grow.

To adjust to changing client demands and market conditions, cultivate an innovative and continuous improvement culture within your company.

Through data analysis, strategic expansion, and deliberate scaling of operations, you may achieve unprecedented success for your subscription box business while staying true to your core values of quality and client happiness.

CHAPTER NINE

FAQS AND REGULAR QUESTIONS

What Should I Do About Shipment Problems?

Any subscription box company may experience shipping problems from time to time, but they can be successfully avoided with diligent preparation and communication.

To start with, to reduce the possibility of delays or damage during transportation, it is essential to select trustworthy shipping partners or carriers.

Shipping-related issues can be greatly decreased by investigating and choosing reliable shipping firms with a history of on-time deliveries and excellent customer support.

It's also crucial to give subscribers precise and understandable delivery information. Provide tracking numbers, expected delivery timeframes, and any potential delays in plain English via email alerts or website updates.

This lessens subscriber annoyance in the event of unanticipated delivery delays and helps manage subscriber expectations.

It's critical to have a clear policy in place for handling shipping-related issues quickly, such as misplaced or damaged packages.

This could entail providing discounts on subsequent shipments, refunds, or replacements to satisfy customers and preserve their faith in your company.

To improve the entire shipping experience for consumers, it can also be helpful to identify any reoccurring issues and take corrective action by routinely monitoring shipment performance and gathering subscriber feedback.

What Happens If Subscribers Wish To Stop?

Handling subscription cancellations is an inherent aspect of managing a subscription box company, and it is critical to establish unambiguous and simple cancellation procedures.

Provide customers with a simple way to cancel their subscriptions via your website or customer support channels, and make sure that their requests are handled quickly.

By giving customers more control over their subscription experience, flexible subscription options—like month-to-month or prepaid plans with the opportunity to skip or delay deliveries—can help lower the risk of cancellations.

When a subscriber does choose to cancel, it's critical to get feedback to comprehend their motivations. These comments can help avoid cancellations in the future and offer insightful information on areas that need improvement. To entice members to change their minds and renew their subscriptions, think about providing rewards or discounts.

Even if a subscriber chooses to cancel, there's still room for future involvement if you keep lines of contact open with them during the cancellation process and express gratitude for their support.

How Should Refunds And Returns Be Handled?

Sustaining client pleasure and confidence in your subscription box business depends on how well you handle returns and reimbursements.

Start by providing members with easy access to your website or the packaging of your subscription box, along with clear return and refund procedures.

Give precise directions on how to start a return or ask for a refund, along with any special demands or circumstances (such as returning things in their original packaging or within a specified amount of time, for example). To entice clients to keep doing business with you in the future, make the procedure as easy and hassle-free as you can.

Aim to process refunds and returns in a timely and courteous manner. Throughout the process, stay in touch with consumers to let them know how their request is progressing and to address any questions or concerns they may have.

Reducing the number of return requests and raising customer satisfaction levels can both be achieved by putting quality control procedures in place to lessen the possibility of returns for broken or defective goods.

Take proactive measures to resolve any trends or patterns that might point to underlying problems with the product's quality, packing, or consumer expectations by routinely reviewing and analyzing return and refund data. This will help you avoid future returns and refunds.

What legal factors need to be taken into account while operating a subscription box business?

To maintain compliance and safeguard your company, several legal considerations come with operating a subscription box business.

First things first: register your firm with the relevant authorities and decide on the best legal structure for your enterprise, such as a corporation, limited liability company (LLC), partnership, or sole proprietorship.

Make sure you possess all the licenses, permits, and certifications needed to legally run your subscription box business in your area.

These could include business licenses, sales tax permits, permits for handling food (if necessary), and other certifications or laws unique to the industry.

When choosing products for your subscription boxes, be mindful of any copyrights, trademarks, or intellectual property rights attached to the items you choose, and make sure you have the appropriate authorizations or licenses to use them legally.

It is also crucial to put strong data protection and privacy policies in place to protect subscriber information and adhere to data protection laws like the California Consumer Privacy Act (CCPA) and the General Data Protection Regulation (GDPR).

Finally, to make sure that your subscription box business is completely compliance with all applicable rules and regulations and safeguarded from potential legal risks or liabilities, think about speaking with legal specialists or consultants who specialize in business law.

How Can I Successfully Manage My Inventory?

To minimize excess inventory and related expenses and guarantee that you have the products in store to rapidly fulfill subscriber orders, effective inventory management is essential. To effectively estimate demand, manage sales, and keep an eye on stock levels, start by putting inventory tracking methods and software into place.

Analyze subscriber comments and sales data regularly to spot trends and popular products. Then, modify your product offerings and inventory levels accordingly. By doing this, you may lessen the chance of stockouts or overstocking and maximize the mix of your inventory.

To guarantee efficiency and accuracy across the supply chain, clearly define the processes and procedures for receiving, storing, selecting, packing, and shipping inventory.

To reduce excess inventory and storage expenses, think about employing just-in-time inventory management techniques, which entail acquiring things from vendors only when necessary to fulfill subscriber orders.

Conduct physical inventory counts and audits regularly to reconcile inventory records, spot any inconsistencies or possible problems (such as shrinkage or obsolescence), and quickly address them with remedial action.

Streamline inventory operations and lower manual mistake rates by utilizing inventory management tools and technologies including RFID tagging, barcoding, and automated reorder systems.

How can one keep subscribers interested?

The long-term sustainability of your subscription box business depends on your ability to retain subscribers. You may increase subscriber retention rates by putting a few tactics into practice. First and foremost, concentrate on providing value and surpassing subscriber expectations with every box by handpicking premium goods, customized experiences, and special deals or discounts.

To notify subscribers about future boxes, discounts, and the launch of new products, stay in constant contact with them via email updates, newsletters, and social media involvement.

To accommodate different subscriber demands and preferences, provide flexibility and customization options. Some examples of these include the ability to specify product preferences, skip or halt delivery, and upgrade/downgrade subscription tiers.

Attempt to satisfy customers' questions and complaints by offering exceptional customer service and assistance to handle any problems or concerns in a timely and professional manner.

Reward and encourage repeat business, referrals, and a sense of appreciation among subscribers by offering rewards programs, VIP benefits, or referral incentives.

To better understand your subscribers' tastes, expectations, and pain spots, ask them for feedback regularly through surveys or reviews. Then, use this information to keep improving your subscription box products and overall customer experience.

You can optimize the lifetime value of your subscription box clients and boost subscriber happiness and loyalty by putting these suggestions and tactics into practice.

www.ingramcontent.com/pod-product-compliance
Lightning Source LLC
Chambersburg PA
CBHW030047230526
45471CB00003B/983